W9-BSN-676

10/10

DATE DUE

Who invented the word *dinosaur?* Which dinosaur was biggest? What did ancient people think fossils were? Which dinosaur mysteries still haven't been solved?

Dig up the answers to these questions and more in...

Magic Tree House® Research Guide
DINOSAURS

A nonfiction companion to
Dinosaurs Before Dark

It's Jack and Annie's very own guide to the most amazing creatures of all time.
Including:
• Jack and Annie's Dinosaur Hall of Fame
• Bone-hunter mistakes
• Dinosaur neighbors
• Fossil photos
• Dinosaur mysteries
And much more!

Here's what people are saying about the Magic Tree House® Research Guides:

Your Research Guides are a great addition to the Magic Tree House series! I have used Rain Forests *and* Space *as "read-alouds" during science units. Thank you for these!!*—Cheryl M., teacher

My eight-year-old son thinks your books are great—and I agree. I wish my high school students had read the Research Guides when they were his age.
—John F., parent and teacher

And from the Magic Tree House® Web site:

My son loves the Research Guides about knights, pirates, and mummies. He has even asked for a notebook, which he takes with him to the museum for his research.—A parent

The Research Guides have been very helpful to us, as our daughter has an abundance of questions. Please come out with more. They help us help her find the answers to her questions!—An appreciative mom and dad

I love your books. I have a great library at home filled with your books and Research Guides. The [Knights and Castles] *Research Guide really helped me do a report on castles and knights!*—A young reader

Magic Tree House®
Research Guide

DINOSAURS

A nonfiction companion to
Dinosaurs Before Dark

by Will Osborne
and Mary Pope Osborne

illustrated by Sal Murdocca

A STEPPING STONE BOOK™
Random House 🏠 New York

www.randomhouse.com/magictreehouse

Library of Congress Cataloging-in-Publication Data
Osborne, Will. Dinosaurs / by Will Osborne and Mary Pope Osborne ;
illustrated by Sal Murdocca.
    p. cm. — (Magic tree house research guide ; #1)
"A Stepping Stone book."
SUMMARY: Jack and Annie explain about all the different types of dinosaurs.
ISBN 0-375-80296-7 (pbk.) — ISBN 0-375-90296-1 (lib. bdg.)
1. Dinosaurs—Juvenile literature. [1. Dinosaurs.]
I. Osborne, Mary Pope. II. Murdocca, Sal, ill. III. Title. IV. Series.
QE862.D5 O813 2000 567.9—dc21 99-043577

Printed in the United States of America   July 2000   10 9 8 7 6 5 4

Random House, Inc.   New York, Toronto, London, Sydney, Auckland

For Marjorie Osborne

Scientific Consultant:

RAYMOND RYE, Museum Specialist, Department of Paleobiology, National Museum of Natural History, Smithsonian Institution, Washington, D.C.

Education Consultant:

MELINDA MURPHY, Media Specialist, Reed Elementary School, Cypress Fairbanks Independent School District, Houston, Texas.

We would also like to thank Alison Brooks at George Washington University for help with our time line; Helen McGovern at the American Museum of Natural History in New York City for her kind assistance; Paul Coughlin for his imaginative photography; and at Random House, Cathy Goldsmith for her wonderful and creative design, Joy La Brack for her long hours of photo research, Mallory Loehr for her ongoing guidance and support, and most especially, our editor, Shana Corey, for her diligence, insight, and joyful enthusiasm throughout the process of creating this book.

DINOSAURS

Contents

Dear Readers,

We learned a lot about dinosaurs when we went back in time in <u>Dinosaurs Before Dark</u>. When we came home to Frog Creek, we learned even more.

We went to the library. We went to a museum. We checked the Internet.

We were doing <u>research</u>.

Research is like digging for dinosaur bones. You know where to look, but you never know exactly what you're going to find. And in our research, we found a LOT!

We found dinosaur books, dinosaur pictures, and dinosaur videos. We talked to dinosaur experts. We touched dinosaur skeletons. We collected lots and lots of amazing dinosaur facts.

In this book, we're going to share some of our research with you. So get your notebook, get your backpack, and get ready to visit the most amazing creatures that ever lived.

Jack

Annie

1

A World of Dinosaurs

Long ago, the world was very different than it is now. Today, all the land on earth is divided into seven continents. Millions of years ago, there was just one continent.

Scientists have named that ancient continent *Pangaea* (pan-JEE-uh).

Some parts of Pangaea were very dry, like deserts. Other parts were damp and rainy, like swamps. There

A <u>continent</u> is one of the earth's large land masses.

were forests and jungles, plains and mountains, rivers and lakes.

And there were dinosaurs almost everywhere.

Dinosaurs were on earth for over 160 million years. Not all the dinosaurs in this picture were on earth at the same time.

Some dinosaurs were bigger than buildings. Others were as small as ducks.

Some dinosaurs walked on all four legs, like dogs. Others walked on two legs, like people.

Some dinosaurs had many rows of sharp teeth. Others had no teeth at all.

But in some ways, all dinosaurs were alike.

They all were reptiles. They all lived on land. They all laid eggs. They almost all had scaly skins. None of them had fur or hair. And none of them could fly.

Reptiles are cold-blooded, usually scaly-skinned animals. Snakes, turtles, and lizards are reptiles.

Dinosaurs

Reptiles

Lived on land

Laid eggs

Scaly skin—no fur

Couldn't fly

The Age of Reptiles

Scientists believe that the first dinosaur was born over 225 million years ago. They believe the last dinosaurs died about 65 million years ago. That means there were dinosaurs on earth for more than 160 million years!

All the dinosaurs lived during what is called the *Mesozoic* (mez-uh-ZO-ick) *Era.* Scientists also call this time the "Age of Reptiles" or the "Age of Dinosaurs."

Scientists divide the Mesozoic Era into three parts, or periods. The first is the *Triassic* (try-AA-sick) *Period.* The middle is the *Jurassic* (jur-AA-sick) *Period.* The last is the *Cretaceous* (krih-TAY-shus) *Period.*

Different kinds of dinosaurs lived in each period. The ones we know best today lived during the Jurassic and Cretaceous periods. That's over 60 million years before the first human was born.

So how can we know about dinosaurs if

no human has ever actually seen one?
We know about them because they left

MESOZOIC ERA

TRIASSIC PERIOD
251–203 million years ago

JURASSIC PERIOD
203–146 million years ago

Stegosaurus

Coelophysis

A TIME

Eoraptor
Dawn of Dinosaurs

Diplodocus

their bones and teeth and footprints
all over the world.

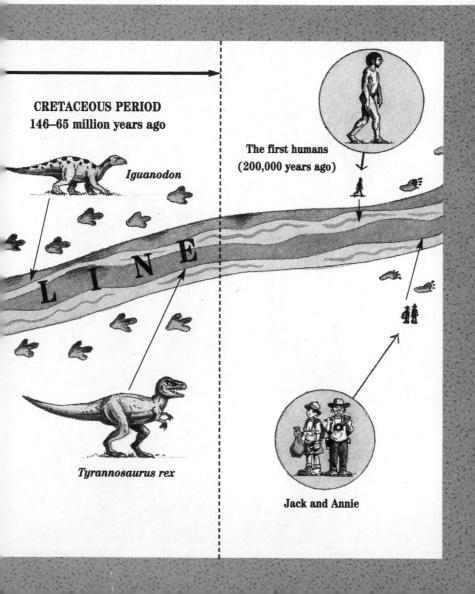

CRETACEOUS PERIOD
146–65 million years ago

Iguanodon

The first humans
(200,000 years ago)

LINE

Tyrannosaurus rex

Jack and Annie

2

Fossils

When people find dinosaur bones today, they aren't really finding bones. They're finding *fossils* (FAH-sulz).

Sometimes a dinosaur died near a stream or river. If the stream or river overflowed, the dinosaur's body would be covered by mud and sand. Over millions of years, the mud and sand turned into solid rock. And the dinosaur's skeleton was still inside!

Fossils are any traces of life from a long-ago age.

T. rex fossil found in Montana.

Minerals are natural substances in the earth that do not come from plants or animals.

At the same time, water in the earth seeped into the dinosaur's bones. Minerals in the water turned the bones to stone, too.

So a dinosaur fossil is really a rock that used to be a bone buried inside another rock that used to be some mud and sand!

This is a model of a dinosaur that died at the bottom of a river.

Fossils can tell us a lot about dinosaurs.

Fossil teeth can tell us the kind of food a dinosaur might have eaten. Flat teeth are good for chopping up plants. Sharp, pointed teeth are good for ripping flesh.

Fossil leg bones can tell us how a dinosaur might have walked. Long leg bones are good for fast running. Short, thick leg bones mean the dinosaur probably moved slowly.

Footprint fossils can help us guess how much a dinosaur weighed. Deep footprints mean the dinosaur who made them must have been very heavy. Shallow footprints mean the dinosaur must have been a lightweight.

Footprint fossils can even tell us how

People used to call anything that was dug out of the ground a fossil. (Even potatoes!)

23

dinosaurs traveled. Many footprints going the same way mean the dinosaurs were probably moving in packs or herds. Big footprints beside little footprints mean the dinosaurs may have been traveling with their families.

Everything that we know about dinosaurs we know from fossils. But fossils can only give us clues about dinosaurs and the Age of Reptiles. We have to use our imaginations to picture how these amazing creatures really looked, how they lived, and how they died.

Sets of dinosaur footprints going the same way, like these, are called <u>trackways</u>.

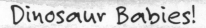

Dinosaur Babies!

Fossils can even tell us about dinosaur eggs, dinosaur nests, and dinosaur babies.

 Some dinosaurs laid their eggs in a circle, like this.

Dinosaur eggs are usually found in nests. But dinosaur nests are not like birds' nests. Most dinosaur nests were dug into sand or mud.

26

Scientists believe some dinosaurs returned to the same nesting grounds year after year.

The biggest dinosaur egg fossils ever found are about the size of a football. But the mother dinosaur that laid them was over 40 feet long!

Why did huge dinosaurs lay small eggs? Scientists think that if dinosaur eggs had been bigger, the shells would have been too thick for baby dinosaurs to break out of.

He's so cute!

3

Dinosaur Hunters

The first people who discovered dinosaur fossils didn't know what they were.

The ancient Chinese thought they came from the skeletons of dragons.

Native Americans thought they came from giant snakes.

Other people who found fossils thought they came from very large elephants—or even giant humans!

In 1822, an English couple named Mary

Ann and Gideon Mantell found some large fossil teeth near their home.

Gideon took the fossils to a museum and looked at them next to teeth from other animals.

Gideon didn't see any teeth that were like the fossils he and Mary Ann had found. He decided the fossils belonged to an animal that didn't live on earth anymore.

An **iguana** is a large South American lizard.

Gideon thought the fossil teeth looked most like giant iguana teeth. So he called the animal they came from an *Iguanodon* (ih-GWAH-nuh-don).

At about the same time, a professor in England named William Buckland was studying the fossil of a very large jawbone. Dr. Buckland decided that this fossil was also from an animal that no longer lived on earth.

He called the creature it came from *Megalosaurus* (MEG-uh-luh-SOAR-us).

That means "big lizard" in Greek.

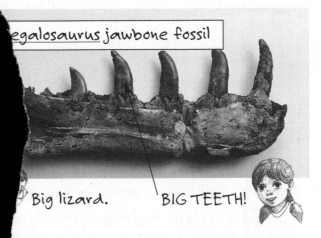

egalosaurus jawbone fossil

Big lizard.   BIG TEETH!

Nearly 20 years later, an English scien-
named Richard Owen studied the
anodon and *Megalosaurus* fossils. He
ld tell that both these creatures were
ally different from any animals still liv-
g on earth. He decided that creatures

like these should have a special name.

Richard Owen chose a name that means "terrifying lizards" in Greek.

The name was *dinosaurs*.

After these early fossil discover

How Dinosaurs Get Their Names

Dinosaur hunters use Latin and words to make up names for the dif kinds of dinosaurs they discover.

Some are named for the place w they were found.

Alamosaurus (AL-uh-muh-SOAR fossils were found near the Alamo, Texas.

Some are named after the person w discovered them.

Marshosaurus (MARSH-uh-SOAR-u

like these should have a special name.

Richard Owen chose a name that means "terrifying lizards" in Greek.

The name was *dinosaurs*.

After these early fossil discoveries,

How Dinosaurs Get Their Names

Dinosaur hunters use Latin and Greek words to make up names for the different kinds of dinosaurs they discover.

Some are named for the place where they were found.

Alamosaurus (AL-uh-muh-SOAR-us) fossils were found near the Alamo, in Texas.

Some are named after the person who discovered them.

Marshosaurus (MARSH-uh-SOAR-us)

that no longer lived on earth.

He called the creature it came from *Megalosaurus* (MEG-uh-luh-SOAR-us). That means "big lizard" in Greek.

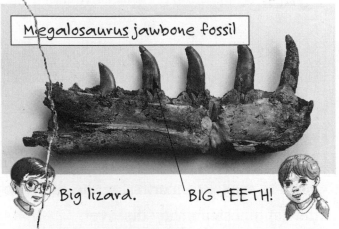

Megalosaurus jawbone fossil

Big lizard. BIG TEETH!

Nearly 20 years later, an English scientist named Richard Owen studied the *Iguanodon* and *Megalosaurus* fossils. He could tell that both these creatures were totally different from any animals still living on earth. He decided that creatures

31

people became very interested in dinosaurs. Scientists wanted more fossils to study. Museums wanted dinosaur skeletons to put on display. There was a race to find more bones!

was named for Othniel Charles Marsh, a famous dinosaur hunter.

Some are named for the way they looked.

Corythosaurus (KOR-ih-thuh-SOAR-us) means "helmet lizard."

Corythosaurus

Sillysaurus!

The Bone Wars

Scientists who study fossils are called *paleontologists* (PAY-lee-un-TAH-luh-jists). Two of the most famous paleontologists were Othniel Charles Marsh and Edward Drinker Cope. They both were Americans who started hunting for fossils in the 1870s.

Marsh

Marsh and Cope were so eager to find new fossils that they became enemies. They hid their discoveries from each other. They sent spies into each other's camps. They even tried to steal each other's bones!

Cope

These two dinosaur hunters fought for 20 years. But their bone battles led to the discovery of more than 130 different kinds of dinosaurs.

Triceratops fossil

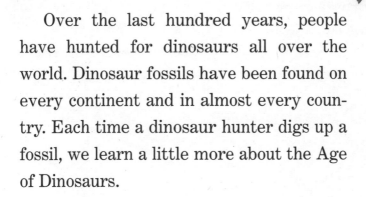

Discovered during the bone wars!

Over the last hundred years, people have hunted for dinosaurs all over the world. Dinosaur fossils have been found on every continent and in almost every country. Each time a dinosaur hunter digs up a fossil, we learn a little more about the Age of Dinosaurs.

35

Bone-Hunting Tools

Dinosaur hunters use lots of tools. Here are some things they always take along when they go digging for fossils.

Magnifying glass—to examine small fossils (like teeth)

Camera—to take pictures of the site and the fossils

Tape measure and ruler—to measure the size of the bones

Field notebook—to keep a record of the bones

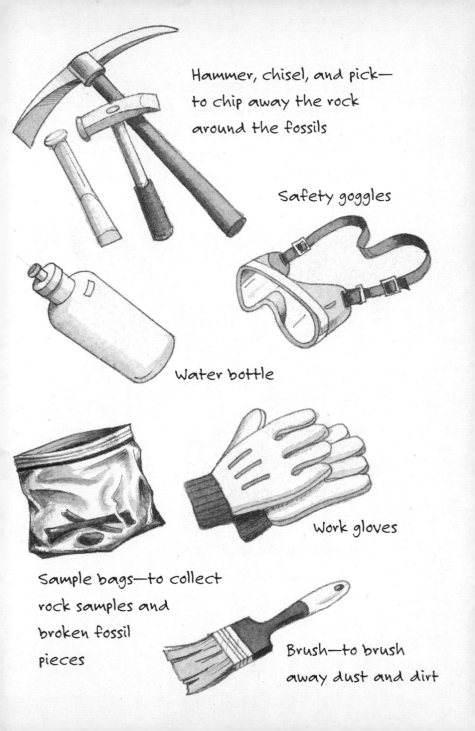

Hammer, chisel, and pick—
to chip away the rock
around the fossils

Safety goggles

Water bottle

Work gloves

Sample bags—to collect
rock samples and
broken fossil
pieces

Brush—to brush
away dust and dirt

Bone-Hunter Mistakes

Even famous dinosaur hunters sometimes goof!

Oops!

The Name Game

For many years people visited museums to see a dinosaur called *Brontosaurus* (BRON-tuh-SOAR-us). But *Brontosaurus* was really the wrong name for this dinosaur. In the late 1800s, a dinosaur hunter put the skull and some other bones of a *Camarasaurus* (kam-AA-ruh-SOAR-us) on the skeleton of an *Apatosaurus* (uh-PAT-uh-SOAR-us). He named his mixed-up dinosaur *Brontosaurus*. It was years before anyone fixed the mistake and corrected the name back to *Apatosaurus*.

The Wrong End

Early in his career, dinosaur hunter Edward Drinker Cope dug up the fossil bones of a giant sea reptile. When he put the bones together, he made a BIG mistake. He mixed up the tail bones with the neck bones. And he stuck the animal's head on the end of its tail!

Horn or Claw?

When Gideon Mantell was studying *Iguanodon* fossils, he thought one of the dinosaur's claws was a giant horn. He drew a picture of an *Iguanodon* with its claw growing out of its snout!

The Wrong Robber

About 80 years ago, dinosaur hunters in Asia found the fossil of a small dinosaur near a nest full of fossilized eggs. They thought the dinosaur was about to raid the nest. So they named it *Oviraptor* (OH-vuh-RAP-tur), which means "egg robber." But paleontologists recently discovered that the *Oviraptor* wasn't stealing another dinosaur's eggs. It was guarding its own eggs so another dinosaur wouldn't steal them!

4

Flesh-eaters

As dinosaur hunters dug up more and more fossils, they realized there were hundreds of different kinds of dinosaurs.

Soon they started sorting them into groups.

The simplest way to sort dinosaurs is by what they ate.

Some dinosaurs ate flesh. Others ate only plants.

Yuck!

Most people call flesh-eating dinosaurs "meat-eaters." But flesh-eaters didn't eat just the meat. They ate everything— brains, bones, guts, and even eyeballs!

<u>Allosaurus</u> fossil

How Do We Know
What Dinosaurs Ate?

Paleontologists use clues from fossils to figure out the kind of food different dinosaurs ate.

Sometimes bones from another animal are found inside the fossil of a dinosaur. That means the dinosaur must have been a flesh-eater.

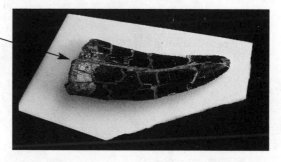

This tooth is long and pointed. It must have been a flesh-eater's.

Some fossil teeth are short and flat. They wouldn't have been good for ripping flesh. So the dinosaur they belonged to must have been a plant-eater.

Sometimes a dinosaur's droppings were fossilized. If the droppings contain seeds, it means the dinosaur was a plant-eater. If they contain ground-up pieces of bone, the dinosaur must have been a flesh-eater.

Paleontologists think all of the very first dinosaurs were flesh-eaters.

The earliest dinosaur fossil ever discovered was from a flesh-eater about the size of a goose. Paleontologists named this dinosaur *Eoraptor* (EE-oh-RAP-tur). *Eoraptor* means "dawn robber." *Eoraptor* lived on earth over 225 million years ago—at the dawn of the age of dinosaurs.

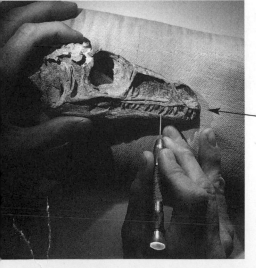

Wow! <u>Eoraptor</u> had a little head, but look at all those teeth!

Paleontologists think *Eoraptor* and other early dinosaurs probably ate insects and small lizards.

Flesh-eating dinosaurs came in many sizes. But they all had a similar shape.

Most of the flesh-eaters walked and ran on their hind legs. They usually had small arms. Most had long, strong tails. Their mouths were full of very sharp teeth.

Flesh-eaters
Walked on hind legs
Small arms
Strong tails
Sharp teeth!

Paleontologists think the flesh-eaters hardly ever stood up straight when they

T. rex fossil

ran. They used their tails for balance and leaned very far forward.

Like this

Flesh-eating dinosaurs had different ways of feeding themselves. Some hunted and killed smaller dinosaurs and other animals. Animals who hunt other animals for food are called *predators*. The animals they hunt are called their *prey*.

Other flesh-eating dinosaurs did not hunt their own food. They lived off the leftovers of the predators. These kinds of animals are called *scavengers*.

Flesh-eating dinosaurs roamed the
rth during all three periods of the Age of
ptiles. They were smart. They were
ce. They were fast. They were proba-
he scariest creatures that ever lived.

ere were hundreds of kinds of
h-eating dinosaurs. Turn the page
some of our favorites.

Coelophysis
(SEE-lo-FY-sis)

This name means "hollow form"

Coelophysis was one of the e...
dinosaurs. Paleontologists thin...
bones and long legs made *Coe*...
a very fast runner.

Fossil hunters in New Mexi...
found dozens of *Coelophysis* ske...
on a ranch called the Ghost R...
Some people say that every nigh...
the Ghost Ranch, *Coelophysis* gh...
come out and dance!

These pictures show our size next to the dinosaur's size.

Coelophysis
(SEE-lo-FY-sis)

Coelophysis was one of the earliest dinosaurs. Paleontologists think light bones and long legs made *Coelophysis* a very fast runner.

Fossil hunters in New Mexico have found dozens of *Coelophysis* skeletons on a ranch called the Ghost Ranch. Some people say that every night on the Ghost Ranch, *Coelophysis* ghosts come out and dance!

These pictures show our size next to the dinosaur's size.

Flesh-eating dinosaurs roamed the earth during all three periods of the Age of Reptiles. They were smart. They were fierce. They were fast. They were probably the scariest creatures that ever lived.

There were hundreds of kinds of flesh-eating dinosaurs. Turn the page for some of our favorites.

THIS WAY

Good vision

Jagged teeth

Strong "finger" claws

Long, strong legs

51

Troodon
(TRO-uh-don)

Paleontologists believe *Troodon* was the smartest dinosaur that ever lived. Its brain was very big for the size of its body.

Troodon's teeth were smaller than a human's, but they had

Strong grip!

52

jagged edges and VERY sharp points.

And *Troodon* was fast! Paleontologists think it could run nearly 30 miles per hour. The fastest humans can run only about 23 miles per hour.

Small teeth—
but sharp!

Claws like hands

Velociraptor
(vuh-LAH-suh-RAP-tur)

Velociraptor had a long, sharp claw on each foot. It could tuck the claw up out of the way when it ran. When it captured its prey, it could bring the claw down to attack it.

In 1971, dinosaur hunters found fossils of a *Velociraptor* along with another dinosaur. The *Velociraptor* was holding the other dinosaur's skull in a tight grip. It looked like it was using its special claw to slice into the other dinosaur's stomach.

About 6 feet long

54

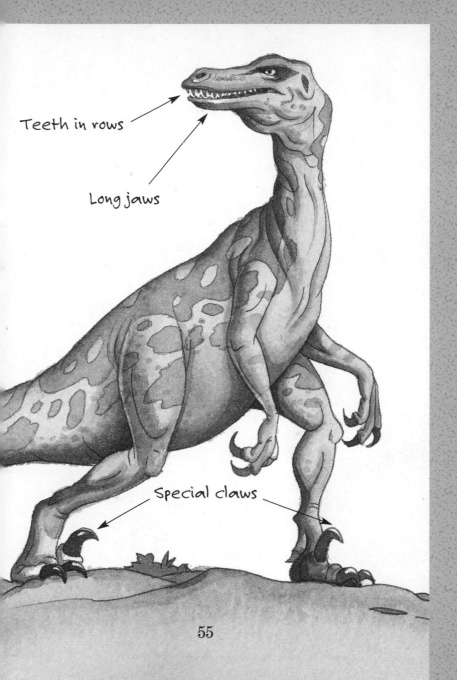

Teeth in rows

Long jaws

Special claws

Baryonyx
(BAA-ree-ON-icks)

This name means "heavy claw"

Baryonyx had a snout like a crocodile's. It had twice as many teeth as most other flesh-eaters. And it had a claw on each "hand" that was so long and sharp it was like a spear.

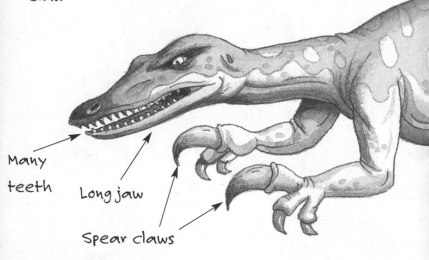

Many teeth

Long jaw

Spear claws

56

Paleontologists think *Baryonyx* must have used its "thumb spears" to catch fish. Why? Because the first *Baryonyx* skeleton ever discovered had a half-eaten fish dinner in its stomach!

Tyrannosaurus rex
(ty-RAN-uh-SOAR-us RECKS)

T. rex is the most famous flesh-eating dinosaur of all time. It had sharp teeth—many were more than six inches long. It had a head the size of a bathtub. One *T. rex* mouthful of food could feed a whole family of humans for weeks.

T. rex had big, strong legs. But its arms were so short they couldn't even reach its mouth. Paleontologists think *T. rex* may have used its arms to help itself stand up after a nap.

Powerful tail

58

BIG head

Almost 20 feet tall

BIG mouth

BIG teeth

Tiny arms

Strong legs

Giganotosaurus
(jig-uh-NOT-uh-SOAR-us)

This name means "giant lizard of the south"

So far, only one *Giganotosaurus* skeleton has been found. But paleontologists believe this giant flesh-eater was even bigger than *T. rex!*

Big skull

60

Dinosaur hunters are looking for more *Giganotosaurus* skeletons. It's possible that when they find them, *Giganotosaurus* will replace *T. rex* as king of the flesh-eating dinosaurs.

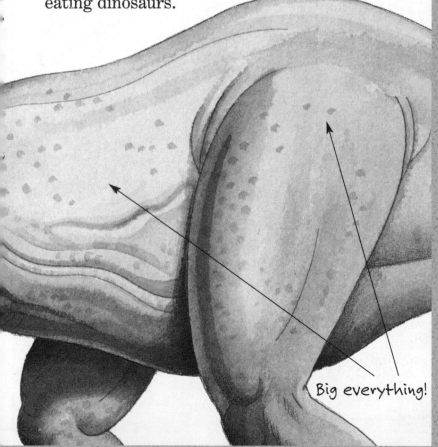

Big everything!

Sauropod fossil

5

Plant-eaters

The first, the fastest, and the smartest dinosaurs were flesh-eaters. But the very biggest dinosaurs ate nothing but plants.

The first plant-eating dinosaurs appeared on earth several million years after the first flesh-eaters. Like the flesh-eaters, plant-eaters lived during all three periods of the Age of Reptiles.

There were many more kinds of plant-eaters than flesh-eaters. Some made meals out of ferns and bushes. Others were tall enough to eat leaves from the tops of trees. But none of them hunted other animals for food.

Plant-eaters
Many different kinds
Some very tall
Some short
None hunted other
   animals

Plant-eaters
lived during all
three periods
of the Age of
Dinosaurs.

Not all these
plant-eaters lived
at the same time.

The biggest plant-eaters were the *sauropods* (SOAR-uh-pods). The sauropods left footprints as big as truck tires. They have names that mean things like "monster lizard" and "titanic lizard."

For many years, paleontologists thought the biggest dinosaur of all time was a sauropod called *Brachiosaurus* (BRACK-ee-uh-SOAR-us).

Brachiosaurus was as long as three school buses. But now, fossil hunters have found bones of three dinosaurs that were even bigger:

Big
- *Supersaurus* (SOO-per-SOAR-us), which means "super lizard";
- *Ultrasaurus* (ULL-truh-SOAR-us), which means "extreme lizard";

Really big
- *Seismosaurus* (SIZE-muh-SOAR-us), which means "earth-shaking lizard."

Really, really big!

66

We don't know much about these giant sauropods because only a few of their bones have ever been found. But some paleontologists think *Seismosaurus* might have been over 150 feet long—as long as *six* school buses!

Was *Seismosaurus* the biggest dinosaur of all? No one knows. Dinosaur hunters discover new fossils every year. It's possible that any day they'll dig up the bones of an even bigger giant.

Turn the page to see some of our favorite plant-eaters!

THIS WAY

Our Favorite Plant-eaters

Stegosaurus
(STEG-uh-SOAR-us)

Stegosaurus was about the size of a mini-van. It had four long spikes on the end of its tail. It had big, flat plates growing out of its back.

This name means "roofed lizard"

    Stegosaurus had a very small head. For many years, most books described *Stegosaurus* as having a brain the size of a golf ball. But paleontologists now think that *Stegosaurus*'s brain looked more like a hot dog!

Stegosaurus brain

Hot dog

Long tail spikes

Flat back plates

Huge
body

Tiny
head

69

Ankylosaurus
(an-KEE-luh-SOAR-us)

Ankylosaurus was the size of an army tank—and built like one! Its body and head were covered with armor. The armor was made of bone. It protected *Ankylosaurus* from flesh-eating dinosaurs like *T. rex*.

Heavy armor

Spikes for protection

70

Ankylosaurus had a big club on the end of its tail. Paleontologists think *Anky-losaurus* used its tail club to smash the feet and legs of any dinosaur that tried to attack it.

Tail club

Edmontosaurus
(ED-mont-uh-SOAR-us)

Edmontosaurus also used to be called *Anatosaurus* (uh-NAT-uh-SOAR-us).

Edmontosaurus had a bill like a duck's. It also had over a thousand teeth! When any of its teeth wore out, new ones grew to replace them.

Strong legs

72

Paleontologists believe that *Edmontosaurus* took good care of their babies. They protected their nests. They gathered food for the babies to eat. They probably looked after their babies until they were old enough to look after themselves.

1,000 teeth in mouth!

Bill like a duck's

Triceratops
(try-SEHR-uh-tops)

Triceratops had a face like a scary Halloween mask. It had a beak like a parrot's. It had three long horns.

Paleontologists believe that *Triceratops* used their horns mostly to fight off other dinosaurs that were trying to eat them. But they also think that sometimes two male *Triceratops* would lock horns and fight with each other over a female.

74

Three horns

Neck shield
(called a <u>frill</u>)

Beak like
a parrot's

75

Diplodocus
(dip-LOD-uh-kus)

Diplodocus was a long, skinny sauropod. It had a long tail and very strong legs. Some paleontologists believe *Diplodocus* could balance on its back legs and its tail, then stretch up to eat from the very tops of trees.

Diplodocus ate almost all the time! Its mouth was so small compared with its body that it had to take hundreds of bites to make a meal.

VERY long tail

Small head

Very long neck

Small mouth

Strong legs

77

Brachiosaurus
(BRACK-ee-uh-SOAR-us)

This name means "arm lizard" (named for long front legs)

Brachiosaurus looked a little bit like a giraffe. It had a very long neck and a small head. It had front legs that were longer than its back legs. But *Brachiosaurus* was twice as tall as a giraffe. And its nostrils were on the top of its head!

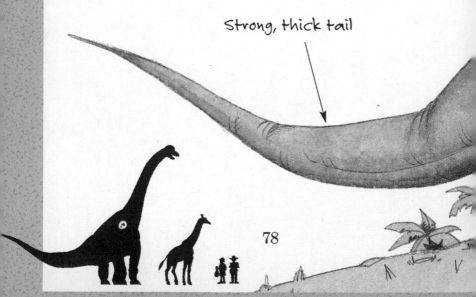

Strong, thick tail

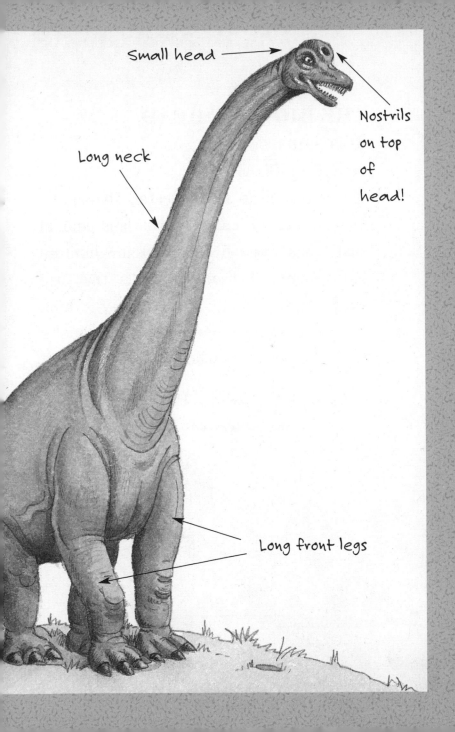

Small head

Nostrils on top of head!

Long neck

Long front legs

THE BIGGEST HEAD
Torosaurus
(TOAR-uh-SOAR-us)

Torosaurus was a plant-eater. It had the biggest head of any known land animal that has ever lived. Dinosaur hunters have found *Torosaurus* skulls that are over eight feet long! They think *Torosaurus*'s head must have been about a third the size of its whole body.

If Annie's head were a third the size of her body, she would look like this

80

THE LONGEST NECK
Mamenchisaurus
(mah-MENCH-ih-SOAR-us)

Mamenchisaurus was also a plant-eater. It had the longest neck of any of the dinosaurs. *Mamenchisaurus*'s neck was about 33 feet long. That's nearly half the length of its entire body.

If Jack's neck were half the length of his body, he would look like this

81

THE BIGGEST EYES
Dromiceiomimus
(drom-uh-SEE-uh-MIME-us)
Dromiceiomimus was a flesh-eater. It was about the size of an ostrich and had eyeballs as big as oranges.

If Annie's eyes were as big as oranges, she would look like this

THE LONGEST NAME

Micropachycephalosaurus

(MY-cro-PACK-ee-SEF-uh-lo-SOAR-us)

Micropachycephalosaurus was a small plant-eater discovered in China. Its long name means "tiny *(micro)*, thick *(pachy)*, head *(cephalo)*, lizard *(saurus)*."

His real name is <u>Glassesandbackpackboy</u>

6

Sea Monsters and Flying Creatures

Dinosaurs ruled the earth during the Age of Reptiles. But they weren't the only creatures around. Dinosaur hunters have also found fossils of many strange flying and swimming reptiles that lived at the same time.

Flying reptiles are called *pterosaurs* (TEH-ruh-soars). *Pterosaur* is Greek for "winged lizard."

Pterosaurs had wings made of skin and

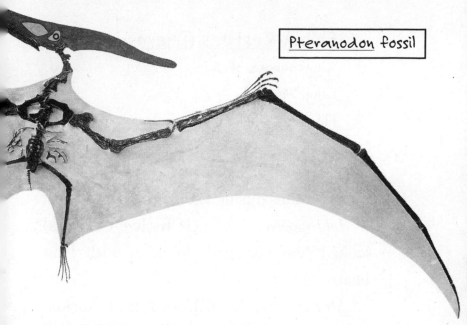

Pteranodon fossil

bone. Each wing was attached to a very long "finger." The finger stretched all the way from the pterosaur's "hand" to the tip of its wing. Sometimes the finger was more than ten feet long!

Paleontologists think most pterosaurs "flew" by stretching out their wings and floating on the wind.

Flying Reptiles (Pterosaurs)
Wings made of skin
Long "finger"
Floated on the wind

There were also several types of swimming reptiles during the Age of Dinosaurs.

Ichthyosaurs (ICK-thee-uh-soars) looked like big-eyed dolphins with long beaks.

Mosasaurs (MOZE-ah-soars) looked like giant swimming lizards with long toes and webbed feet.

Plesiosaurs (PLEE-zee-uh-soars) did not look like *anything* on earth today.

Some plesiosaurs had short necks and long jaws, like crocodiles. Others had long necks and small heads, like the giant sauropod dinosaurs.

Sea Reptiles
Ichthyosaurs
Mosasaurs
Plesiosaurs

Plesiosaur fossil

Turn the page to see some of our
favorite flying creatures
and sea monsters
in action!

THIS WAY

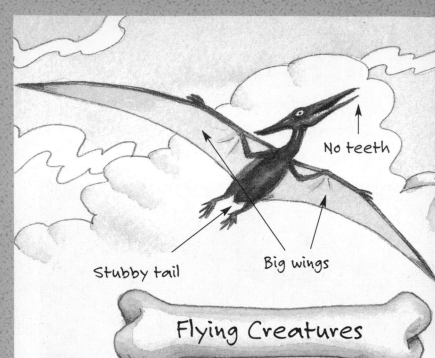

No teeth

Stubby tail

Big wings

Flying Creatures

Pteranodon
(teh-RAN-uh-don)

This name means "toothless flier"

Pteranodon had a long beak and a long, bony crest on the back of its head. It probably needed the crest to help balance its beak when it was swooping down to catch fish.

88

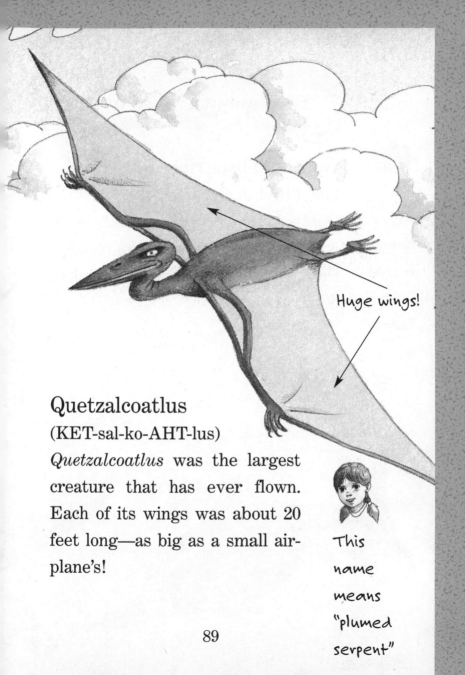

Huge wings!

Quetzalcoatlus
(KET-sal-ko-AHT-lus)

Quetzalcoatlus was the largest creature that has ever flown. Each of its wings was about 20 feet long—as big as a small airplane's!

This name means "plumed serpent"

Ophthalmosaurus
(ahf-THAL-muh-SOAR-us)

Ophthalmosaurus was an ichthyosaur with very large eyes. Paleontologists think its big eyes helped it see in dark ocean water.

This name means "eye lizard"

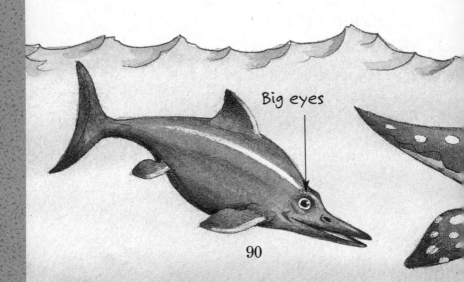

Big eyes

90

Elasmosaurus
(ee-LAZ-muh-SOAR-us)

Elasmosaurus was a plesiosaur. *Elasmosaurus*'s neck made up more than half the length of its entire body.

Paleontologists think that *Elasmosaurus* may have hunted for food by swimming around with its neck sticking out of the water, looking for fish near the surface.

This name means "plated lizard"

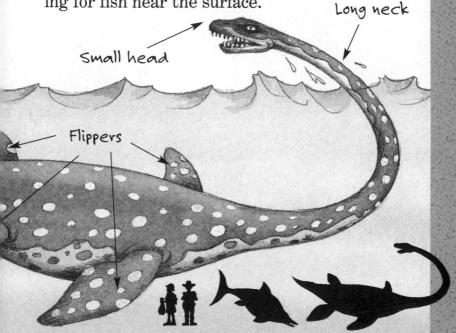

Small head

Long neck

Flippers

7

What Happened to the Dinosaurs?

Dinosaurs lived on earth for millions and millions of years. Then they vanished completely.

What happened? Why did they all die? No one really knows for sure.

Scientists call an idea that hasn't been proved a *theory*. There are a few theories that explain why dinosaurs are no longer on earth.

The Changing Climate Theory

For many years, most paleontologists thought the dinosaurs disappeared very slowly. They thought they died out because of *climate changes*.

Paleontologists who believe this theory think that the earth's climate began to change at the end of the Age of Reptiles. As the climate changed, the world of the dinosaurs changed, too.

Paleontologists who believe the changing climate theory think that many dinosaurs couldn't adapt to the changes.

They think that over the years, more and more dinosaurs died, until there were none left. They had become *extinct*.

The Asteroid Theory

The changing climate theory was popular for a long time. But many paleontologists now have another theory. They think the dinosaurs were wiped out much faster. Their theory is called the *asteroid theory*.

An *asteroid* is a rock from outer space. Paleontologists who believe the asteroid theory think a big asteroid hit the earth at the end of the Age of Reptiles. They think the asteroid was over five miles wide.

Wow! That's as big as a whole town.

An asteroid that size would kill all the animals within hundreds of miles of where it landed. When it hit the earth, it would send a giant cloud of dust and smoke and ash flying into the air.

The cloud would stay in the air for years. It would block out most of the sunlight.

Without sunlight, the earth would get colder. Plants would die. Some dinosaurs would freeze to death. Others would starve. Soon they would all be gone.

For many years, paleontologists who believed the asteroid theory wondered where the giant asteroid might have hit the earth.

Now they think they have found the spot.

A <u>crater</u> is a dent in the earth.

Scientists have discovered a crater in the Gulf of Mexico. The crater is 120 miles wide. It is buried half a mile deep in the earth under the ocean.

The crater is full of the same kinds of minerals that have been found where smaller asteroids have landed.

Today, most paleontologists believe

the asteroid theory. But it is still just a theory.

We may never know for sure why dinosaurs vanished from the earth. The death of these strange and wonderful creatures is one of the biggest mysteries of all time.

Turn the page for more dinosaur mysteries.

More Dinosaur Mysteries

Paleontologists have been studying dinosaur fossils for almost 200 years. But there are some things fossils just can't tell us...

Case #1: Seeing Red!

What color were dinosaurs? Were they brown and gray? Or were they bright red? Green? Yellow? Were they spotted? Did they have stripes?

Fossils can't answer these questions. But many paleontologists think dinosaurs might have been as colorful as today's lizards and snakes.

Case #2: An Age-old Riddle

How many years did a dinosaur live? Ten years? Thirty years? No one knows for certain. Many paleontologists think some dinosaurs lived to be over a hundred years old!

Case #3: Two-ton Tooters

What kinds of sounds did dinosaurs make? Did they roar like lions? Did they honk like geese? Hiss? Chirp? Growl?

Paleontologists can only guess, based on the shapes of dinosaurs' heads and bodies. Some dinosaurs had bony tubes on their skulls. Paleontologists think they might have tooted their tubes like bugles!

8

Dinosaur Neighbors

Dinosaurs are no longer on earth. But several kinds of creatures who lived among the dinosaurs are still with us.

Lizards were the favorite meal of many small flesh-eaters. Paleontologists think today's lizards are almost exactly the same as the ones that lived during the Age of Reptiles.

The first turtles were also on earth with the dinosaurs. They looked a lot like turtles today—except some were much bigger. Paleontologists have discovered the fossil of one turtle that was over 12 feet long!

Stupendemys fossil

That's a BIG turtle!

Crocodiles also lived during the time of dinosaurs. Most were about the same size as crocodiles today. But dinosaur hunters have found one crocodile skull fossil in Texas more than six feet long. That means the crocodile was probably five times as big as crocodiles today!

Phobosuchus skull fossil

And a BIG crocodile!

The creatures today that are most like dinosaurs, though, are not lizards or turtles or crocodiles.

They are small creatures you see every day. They're right outside your window or in your backyard.

They're birds!

Dinosaur Neighbors
Lizards

Turtles

Crocodiles

BIRDS!

Paleontologists think the first birds appeared on earth during the Jurassic Period. They think birds are closely related to flesh-eating dinosaurs. Some even think there was once a creature that was half bird and half dinosaur!

In 1861, workers in Germany dug up the fossil of a small skeleton. The skeleton looked as if it belonged to a flesh-eating dinosaur. But when they looked closely at the stone around the fossilized bones, they saw imprints of feathers. The dinosaur had wings!

Paleontologists named this creature *Archaeopteryx* (AHR-kee-OP-tur-icks). That means "ancient wing." Today, the *Archaeopteryx* fossil is one of the most valuable fossils in all the world.

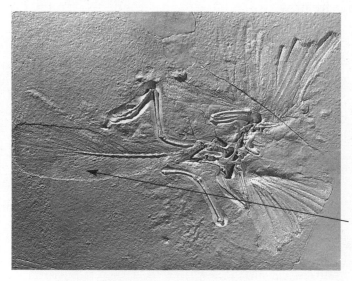

Oh, ma
Fossil
feather

How did birds, crocodiles, turtles, and lizards stay alive when the dinosaurs all died out?

No one knows.

It's another mystery the dinosaur hunters and paleontologists of the future will have to solve.

It's possible the answer is out there right now...

buried in the mud somewhere...

waiting...

for *you* to dig it up.

Doing More Research

If you want to become a dinosaur expert, reading this book is just the beginning. There's lots more you can do to learn about dinosaurs.

Part of the fun of research is seeing how many different sources you can explore.

Turn the page for some dinosaur research tips.

THIS WAY

Books

Most libraries and bookstores have a lot of dinosaur books.

Here are some things to remember when you're using a book for research:

1. You don't have to read the whole book. Check the table of contents and the index to find the topics you're interested in.
2. Write down the name of the book. When you take notes, make sure you write down the name of the book in your notebook so you can find it again.
3. Never copy exactly from a book. When you learn something new from a book, put it in your own words.
4. Find out when the book was written. We learn more about dinosaurs all the

time. Make sure the book you're using isn't too old. A librarian or teacher can help you find out when a book was written.

Here are some good dinosaur books that were written in the last few years:

- *The Best Book of Dinosaurs* by Christopher Maynard
- *Dinosaur Worlds* by Don Lessem
- *Dinosaurs* a *Reader's Digest* Pathfinders book
- *Dinosaurs and Other Archosaurs* by Peter Zallinger
- *The New Book of Dinosaurs* by Dr. David Unwin
- *On the Trail of Incredible Dinosaurs* by William Lindsay

Museums

Science and natural history museums are great places to do dinosaur research. Most large ones have dinosaur skeletons on display. Even very small ones will probably have fossil displays.

When you go to a museum:

1. Be sure to take your notebook!
Write down anything you see that catches your interest. Draw pictures, too!
2. Ask questions.
There are almost always people at a museum who can help you find what you're looking for.
3. Check the museum calendar.
Many museums have special events and activities just for kids!

Here are some museums around the
country with good dinosaur displays:

- American Museum of Natural History
  New York, New York
- Carnegie Museum of Natural History
  Pittsburgh, Pennsylvania
- Lawrence Hall of Science
  University of California
  Berkeley, California
- North Carolina Museum of Life and
  Sciences
  Durham, North Carolina
- Science Museum of Minnesota
  St. Paul, Minnesota
- Smithsonian Institution
  Washington, D.C.

Videos

Most dinosaur movies are *fiction*. That means someone made up the story. They probably made up a lot about dinosaurs that isn't true. But there are some videos that tell real stories.

They're called *nonfiction*.

Check your library or video store for nonfiction videos about dinosaurs.

Here are two really good nonfiction dinosaur videos:

- *Dinosaur Hunters*
  from National Geographic Video
- *The Dinosaurs*
  (four-video set)
  from PBS Home Video

CD-ROMs

CD-ROMs usually have plenty of facts plus fun activities. They can help you learn more about fossils, dinosaurs, and dinosaur hunters.

Here are three of our favorite dinosaur CD-ROMs:

- *Dinosaur Hunter*
  from DK Interactive Learning
- *The Dinosaur Hunter's Kit*
  (CD-ROM plus activity kit)
  from Running Press
- *A World of Dinosaurs*
  (five-piece CD-ROM set)
  from Countertop Software

The Internet

There are many Web sites about dinosaurs. Most of them are *updated* often. That means they have the very latest research.

Here are a few dinosaur Web sites. Ask your teacher or your parents to help you find more:

- www.clpgh.org/cmnh/discovery/index.html
- kids.discovery.com/KIDS/
- www.enchantedlearning.com
- www.nmnh.si.edu/paleo/dino

Field Trips

There are some places where you can actually see dinosaur fossils still buried in the earth—and dinosaur hunters at work.

If you live or vacation near one of these places, check out the fossils:

- Dinosaur National Monument
  Dinosaur, Colorado
- Dinosaur Provincial Park
  Patricia, Alberta, Canada
- Museum of the Rockies
  Montana State University
  Bozeman, Montana
- The Wyoming Dinosaur Center
  Thermopolis, Wyoming

Good luck!

Index

diet of, 43–46

disappearance of,
    93–97

eggs of, 16, 26–27

footprints of,
    23–25

legs of, 23, 46, 58

lifespan of, 99

naming of, 32–33

nests of, 26–27

skin of, 16

sounds made by,
    99

teeth of, 23, 30,
    31, 44, 46, 52,
    58

see also
    individual species
    names

Diplodocus, 76–77

Dromiceiomimus,
    82

Edmontosaurus,
    72–73

Elasmosaurus, 91

Eoraptor, 18, 45–46

extinction, 94

flesh-eaters, 42–61,
    63, 82

fossils, 21–27, 29–31,
    33–37, 98,
    104–105

Giganotosaurus,
    60–61

ichthyosaurs,
    86–87, 90

iguana, 30

Iguanodon, 19,
    30–31, 40

Jurassic Period, 17, 18, 104

lizards, 100, 101

Mamenchisaurus, 81
Mantell, Gideon, 30, 40
Mantell, Mary Ann, 29–30
Marsh, Othniel Charles, 33, 34
Marshosaurus, 32–33
Megalosaurus, 31
Mesozoic Era, 17
Micropachy-cephalosaurus, 83
minerals, 22
mosasaurs, 86, 87

Ophthalmosaurus, 90
Oviraptor, 41
Owen, Richard, 31–32

paleontologists, 34, 36–37
  tools of, 36–37
Pangaea, 13–14
plant-eaters, 45, 63–79, 80, 81, 83
plesiosaurs, 86, 87, 91
predators, 48
prey, 48
Pteranodon, 88
pterosaurs, 84–85, 86, 88, 89

Quetzalcoatlus, 89

How long did it take to become a knight?

What was the food like in castles?

How did it feel to wear armor? Did horses wear armor, too?

Find out what life in medieval times was really like with Jack and Annie's

**Magic Tree House®
Research Guide #2**

KNIGHTS AND CASTLES

A nonfiction companion to
The Knight at Dawn

And coming soon...

**Magic Tree House®
Research Guide #3**

MUMMIES
AND PYRAMIDS

A nonfiction companion to
Mummies in the Morning

and

**Magic Tree House®
Research Guide #4**

PIRATES

A nonfiction companion to
Pirates Past Noon

Are you a fan of the
Magic Tree House® series?

Visit our
MAGIC TREE HOUSE®

Web site at
www.randomhouse.com/magictreehouse

Exciting sneak previews of the next book.
Games, puzzles, and other fun activities.
Contests with super prizes.
And much more!

Other books by Mary Pope Osborne and Will Osborne:

Picture books:

Kate and the Beanstalk by Mary Pope Osborne

Mo and His Friends by Mary Pope Osborne

Moonhorse by Mary Pope Osborne

Rocking Horse Christmas by Mary Pope Osborne

First chapter books:

The *Magic Tree House®* series by Mary Pope Osborne

For middle-grade readers:

Adaline Falling Star by Mary Pope Osborne

American Tall Tales by Mary Pope Osborne

The Deadly Power of Medusa by Mary Pope Osborne
    and Will Osborne

Favorite Greek Myths by Mary Pope Osborne

Favorite Medieval Tales by Mary Pope Osborne

Favorite Norse Myths by Mary Pope Osborne

Jason and the Argonauts by Mary Pope Osborne
    and Will Osborne

Joe Magarac by Will Osborne

The Life of Jesus in Masterpieces of Art
    by Mary Pope Osborne

Mermaid Tales from Around the World
by Mary Pope Osborne
My Brother's Keeper by Mary Pope Osborne
My Secret War by Mary Pope Osborne
One World, Many Religions by Mary Pope Osborne
Spider Kane and the Mystery Under the May-Apple
(#1) by Mary Pope Osborne
Spider Kane and the Mystery at Jumbo Nightcrawler's
(#2) by Mary Pope Osborne
Standing in the Light by Mary Pope Osborne
13 Ghosts: Strange but True Stories by Will Osborne

For young-adult readers:
Haunted Waters by Mary Pope Osborne

Where have you traveled in the Magic Tree House®?

- ❏ #1: Dinosaurs Before Dark
- ❏ #2: The Knight at Dawn
- ❏ #3: Mummies in the Morning
- ❏ #4: Pirates Past Noon
- ❏ #5: Night of the Ninjas
- ❏ #6: Afternoon on the Amazon
- ❏ #7: Sunset of the Sabertooth
- ❏ #8: Midnight on the Moon
- ❏ #9: Dolphins at Daybreak
- ❏ #10: Ghost Town at Sundown
- ❏ #11: Lions at Lunchtime
- ❏ #12: Polar Bears Past Bedtime
- ❏ #13: Vacation Under the Volcano
- ❏ #14: Day of the Dragon King
- ❏ #15: Viking Ships at Sunrise
- ❏ #16: Hour of the Olympics
- ❏ #17: Tonight on the *Titanic*
- ❏ #18: Buffalo Before Breakfast
- ❏ #19: Tigers at Twilight
- ❏ #20: Dingoes at Dinnertime
- ❏ #21: Civil War on Sunday
- ❏ #22: Revolutionary War on Wednesday

A STEPPING STONE BOOK™

Great authors write great books...
for fantastic first reading experiences!

Grades 1–3

Duz Shedd series
  by Marjorie Weinman Sharmat
Junie B. Jones series by Barbara Park
Magic Tree House® series
  by Mary Pope Osborne
Marvin Redpost series by Louis Sachar

Clyde Robert Bulla
The Chalk Box Kid
The Paint Brush Kid
White Bird

Jackie French Koller
Mole and Shrew All Year Through

Jerry Spinelli
Tooter Pepperday
Blue Ribbon Blues: A Tooter Tale

Grades 2–4

A to Z Mysteries series by Ron Roy
Katie Lynn Cookie Company series
  by G. E. Stanley

Polly Berrien Berends
The Case of the Elevator Duck

Ann Cameron
Julian, Dream Doctor
Julian, Secret Agent
Julian's Glorious Summer

Adèle Geras
Little Swan

**Stephanie Spinner &
Jonathan Etra**
Aliens for Breakfast
Aliens for Lunch
Aliens for Dinner

Gloria Whelan
Next Spring an Oriole
Silver
Hannah
Night of the Full Moon
Shadow of the Wolf

Grades 3–5

FICTION
Magic Elements Quartet
  by Mallory Loehr
#1: Water Wishes
#2: Earth Magic
#3: Wind Spell

Spider Kane Mysteries
  by Mary Pope Osborne
#1: Spider Kane and the Mystery Under
  the May-Apple
#2: Spider Kane and the Mystery at
  Jumbo Nightcrawler's

NONFICTION
Thomas Conklin
The *Titanic* Sinks!

Elizabeth Cody Kimmel
Balto and the Great Race

MARY POPE OSBORNE and WILL OSBORNE have been married for a number of years and live in New York City with their Norfolk terrier, Bailey. Mary is the author of over fifty books for children, and Will has worked for many years in the theater as an actor, director, and playwright. Together they have co-authored two books of Greek mythology.

Here's what Will and Mary had to say about working together on *Dinosaurs:*

"For years, we have both loved using our imaginations to visit and explore new worlds. Working on the Magic Tree House nonfiction books gives us the opportunity to make these journeys together. Like Jack and Annie, we loved researching dinosaurs. The most fun part of our research was visiting the American Museum of Natural History, in New York City. Walking among fossils of *Tyrannosaurus rex*, *Triceratops*, and *Pteranodon* took us back 200 million years. That's not a bad way to time-travel and still be home before dark, is it?"